Warrior / Queen

Warrior/Queen

22 love poems

by Daphne Rose Kingma

First Edition 2016

All inquiries and permission requests should be addressed to the Editor,
Valley Green Press
PO Box 5244,
Santa Barbara, California 93150

Cover design by Daphne Rose Kingma and Bo von Hohenlohe.
Book production by Bo von Hohenlohe Productions.
Cover art: "Adieu" by Sulamith Wülfing,
Permission of Blue Star Communications, Orinda, Caifornia
Author photo by Javiera Estrada.

ISBN: 978-0-692-79276-6
Library of Congress Control Number: 2016917263

For M

you loosen
my tears
like God loosens the rain
from the clouds

and I
shall rejoice
when my tears
fall

into the bowl
of your hands

Someday you will meet someone unexpectedly
and you will be surprised

You're the chairman of the department
he's the graduate assistant

You're the editor-in-chief
she's the foreign correspondent

You're about to be married
he's about to be divorced

You find yourself contemplating a relationship
convention says you should not pursue

And then memory takes over...

I seem to have loved you
in numberless forms, numberless times…
in life after life, in age after age,
forever.
—*Rabindranath Tagore*

Table of Contents

1

With Us

I have joy with him
and comfort of speech
and bliss in the body.

My white wings rise
as I walk.

We are woven
of one soul.

We move through our
rooms and the passages
of time with great ease
and beauty.

It is my honor, always
to behold him.

The smell of blood
rises, and the scent
of broken bones.

For me, he reaches
out his hand.

His hands: so
beautiful.

2

I Shall Once Again Serve Him

I am honored to be God's
maid-servant in this matter.
I am honored to be my beloved's
Hathor. I am honored
to bind up his wounds:

> *how he came to me again*
> *this time with his skull cracked*
> *open and tears of stone riveted to*
> *the silver skin of his heart*

I am honored
to shew him his grandeur.
I am honored that the white
bird flies for us.

But who will love me,
O Lord, while I am
serving this honor?

Who will brush back
the hair from my brow
and anoint my pink
lips with kisses?

Who will lift my arms
in the dance? Who will
follow the movement
of my white skirts
in the wind?

When my heart is heavy
with the ancient sorrows,
who will gather me home?

Who will hold me in
the dark hours, bathing
my cathedral in the
nectar of his scepter?

Who will sing to me?

Who will ride me
home on his horse
while the sun falls
like a wild plum
against the blue knife
of the horizon?

Who will grow old
with me?

Who will remember
the shape of my mouth
when I was still young,
the fainting blues of my
eyes, and the perfect names
of all my sorrows?

I will carry him, O Lord.

I will lay him out on the
table and wrap his wounds
with white cloths. With knives
will I scrape all the pain from
his shoulders, from the
places between his
ribs, from his hands
and the might of his
calves, till his cry
howls up and his
tears fall down.

I will wrap him
in incense, in petals of
roses, and sandalwood and
myrrh, till all his old wounds
be wet with the perfume
of blossoms, with the
fragrance of dancing,
with the color of
new songs.

With white gauzes
will I bind him, and
with flowers, with
many colored petals to
his skin, that his heart may
remember the shape of his
face before his parents
beheld him, the peace
of the life he will
come to in time.

For him, O Lord,
will I do this. I will
do this and put my
whole life in your hands.
I will love him and serve
him and heal him, until the
whole world remembers
that in such a serving

a woman becomes a queen.

3

If I Leave My Chair

If I leave my chair,
the chair where I sit
because I know and
you need to find out,
the chair where I tell
all, but never the parts,

the chair where you
sit across from me
feeling the unsaid whole
in all the parts that I tell,
as well as the unspoken
blossoming—

If I leave my chair
we shall both have
names. I, the unnamed
one, will also have a name.
It will be the naming of
flowers and far worlds,
of a goddess escaping
a man, who turned into
a tree. It will be the name
of infinite laurels and roses

and it will bloom on your lips
with the sound of the fragrance
of stamens, of deeply petalled
embedded perfumes.

If I leave my chair
you will know your true
beauty. My hands will
explain it to you, tracing
that trout that perpetually swims
on your shoulder, and the polished
stones of your shoulders themselves
and your immemorial warrior hands
and the two black centipedes of hair
above your eyes, and the tower and
forests I have been forbidden
to see because I must sit
in my chair.

If I leave my chair
you will know your true beauty.
My tongue will announce it to you,
exploring the whorls of your
ears, the narrow sheared
ravine that defines
the promontory
of your lips.

My breath will turn silver,
opalescent, and mirror like a
thousand stars, the sacred blistering
pulse of your heart, and my fingers will
wear like an infinitude of rings,
the small black curls of hair
on your chest.

I will whisper to you.
I will walk across marble
floors dancingly, the loose,
soft risen hems of my dress
fluttering butterfly-like
in the still cool air
of high rooms.

I will speak to you of your power,
of the wars you have warred in and
won—and died in—and of how again and again
(except for that once when I was the brother beside
you, looking up and watching you fall—clatter down
with your sword, with your knitted vest of iron, a second
before the huge hoofs came down and trampled
my own heart shut), I have carried you
home, Oh, Beloved, while the
tears and the blood ran
together, a river of roses,
and my heart was emptied,
scoured of you,
again, again, again.

If I leave my chair
you will know your true
beauty, and I will wonder
if I am beautiful enough
for you, if these pretty lips
which have told so much
truth and so many lies
will be sufficient
to kiss you, kiss your
lips and kiss your eyes,
and speak of the all that
has been kept secret
until now,

If my hands, touching
your cheeks, will satisfy
your sorrows, if the milk
of my thighs will
console you.

If I leave my chair,
we will remember
something, somewhere:

> *Tile roofs and balustrades*
> *the scent of white blossoms*
> *in the golden light of early evening,*
>
> *and how the dog walked, knowing*
> *down the broken granite path.*

If I leave my chair
we will know that
these chairs were not of the
heart. They were not about love.
They were of explaining, of taking
apart thread by thread, the fine
white cloth of the soul, as if
it could be unwoven, and
then woven up again.

When I leave my chair
I will return to my throne
and to the memory of your
face, and the lush obsidian
grandeur of your eyes
and the castle of your
heart. When I leave
my chair, I will serve you

gladly, once again, my Lord.

4

On the Island

I wasn't looking for you.
I came to this island to get away.
But then last night when I laid your book
out on the corner of the bed, your face
bled through the blankets and sheets,
and the scent of raw earth rose up
in the room, and I knew that you
had come for me again.

> *The gates of the garden*
> *opened and you rode in on*
> *your horse, the exact grey or brown*
> *of its legs obscured by the shadows of*
> *walls, high walls and hedges and cobbles,*
> *an iron gate and incandescent white blossoms*
> *lost like stars, in the green geometry of leaves.*
>
> *It was twilight in the blue and golden evening.*
>
> *I could feel your face in the wind,*
> *chords of the tendons in your*
> *legs divinely pulsing, square*
> *hands gathering the reins*
> *and the call of your*
> *eyes to my eyes.*
>
> *I have been waiting for you...*

Now, here, alone
on this island, sifting through lives
in a landscape so unlike the skies
clouds moons olive groves
blunt edges of battlefields
in which before, always,
we kissed

I am waiting again on the balcony,
the air moist and thick, my breath soft
and here, not the virgin grey leaves of olives
but the sound of the waves calls you back—
longing and anguish marching along side by
side, as perfect as a Capricorn accountant's
columns in his books.

The waves rise, turn white and fall
against the edges of the moon,
tides of my blood, my womb,
rising and falling with the blue
iniquity of you, my secret passion,
mystery and haunting brutal
in your piercing through
to me this life again.

I have been waiting forever for you…

> *Cracked orange tiles, smeared*
> *ochre plaster, rustle of silk and crinoline, tall*
> *green louvers closing in autumn and the olives*
> *dropping their grey leaves against the cracked stone of*
> *the garden paths, silver apostrophes floating through air,*
> *falling against the black page of the tilled soil,*
> *damp in the mists of the golden early evening.*

> *I have been waiting for you…*
> *hearing the clap clap clap of your hoofbeats*
> *on the path, my heart still, my thighs a river of song*
> *and in the background my father's voice*
> *calling me in from the balcony.*
> *closing the shutters behind us…*

And how he bought me then—
but of course you never knew it—a
passage on the tall ship, handed it to me
at table like a gift, (it was wrapped in Italian
parchment, wound around with a narrow strip
of brown leather and tied with a crimson ribbon)
and sent me, with trunks full of laces, of
petticoats and bodices and pearls (my
small breasts rising like Persian
melons in their silken wrappings)

to so many cities, hoping that I would
erase you, slice you out of my heart,

but how I saw you always everywhere,
profile traced at midnight in every window,
every mirror, you the shadow over my
shoulder, lines of your hands in every
hand not yours that lifted mine to dance, how
they wondered why they couldn't win me:

> *"So beautiful," they said.*
> *"Yet she remains alone."*

All those ships and all those cities, all that wandering—
and the hand, always the hand and the pen engraving
the pain on the page—

And how finally when he died they called
me back, but you were already gone, how you had ridden,
the maid said, slicing the chicken to ribbons on the wooden table
in the kitchen, how you had ridden a thousand nights
into the courtyard, waiting, breathing, holding a
small bouquet of white blossoms in your hand,
inhaling the absence on the balcony like a
disease that would kill you slowly in the end,

until finding always
no one and nothing—not a note,
nor the trace of a note, nor the fringe
of a ribbon, nor a single lock of hair—
you took yourself off to war

    always the war, always the
    useless futile glorious battle

and smeared your blood on the earth
in a private hieroglyph of pain.

Now, again, there's a distance,
but this time it's only an island,
just a vacation and a man who's not my father
but, anyway, holds me with tight reins.

Always escaping, always running backward
and forward and sideways toward something,
the emptiness in which something—a rose
perhaps—could bring forth a blossom.

Feeling you here, finding you here, seeing your face,
painting your eyes on this renaissance canvas of white cotton
sheets, I sleep, while outside the window the water washes the past
until in the hovering black parenthesis of midnight, the phone
rings and I walk across the orange tiles of the bedroom floor
to pick it up in the dark,

and your voice pours, spills in through the moonlight,
starlight over the tropical ocean:

                "Beloved."

We have oceans of words but none of them
spoken, only these balesfull of tears washing over the ancient
pale intaligoed cameos, landmarks of passion and of longing,
the thousands of lives just like this one in which
we were given only moments

> *the memory of your hands*
> *and of your breathing and of how*
> *your fingers always traced*
> *the long bones of my face*

Tonight my bare feet scrape across the orange
tile floor. I reach for the phone in the dark; you slice
my heart open again with the sound of your voice
and from there over there, wherever you are, you
hear the verdigris wail rising up through
the white thin walls of my throat:

My heart sings but my bones
know that the war calls, the ship
sails, night falls and I will watch once again
                                    as you ride away on your horse

in the perfect golden light of
the murderous early evening

5

Waiting for your Hands

Waiting for your hands—
wearing a short pink dress
tonight, I have tornadoed the bed
where I sit, legs crossed,
toenails painted for summer,

I the great teller of things—
what it means, what to do
about it and when—
have been silenced.

Waiting for your hands
carved fine by the centuries
of stone you carved, and the
swords you carried, the
guns and arrows and
eagle feathers and
knives,

> *sticks of incense, lotus*
> *blossoms, wet leaves and*
> *vines, cathedrals of trees*
> *archways of stone, lead*
> *and glass,*

Waiting for your hands
my skin has become acquainted
with itself, palming the eyes
and the calves and the slow
white hills of my breasts,

> *oils and lotions and potions*
> *and sand and salt and*
> *dry leaves and leather*
> *and bones,*

carnelian and silk
crushed almonds and oatmeal
crinoline and polyurethane
and mud—

Waiting for your hands
my hands held the air
and the barre and
the pen and the skin
of other men's backs
and their boxes of
anger and sorrow.

Waiting for your hands
my heart ravaged other men's
hearts with its holding on and
letting go, with its
tyrannizing indecision.

Waiting for your hands
my hands were photographed,
called beautiful, the white rims
of their nails compared to
the soft white undersides
of doves,

and their gestures celebrated:
"I watched you," said the piano
player at the old hotel, "making
exactly the gestures I have
always wanted to see a
woman making with
her hands."

Waiting for your hands
my hands played the piano
wrote letters and sewed buttonholes
and seams, soldered silver and set
precious stones, polished shoes and cut
wood, clasped the pink scepters of lovers
stroked cats and the beaded
brows of dying soldiers.

Waiting for your hands
to be born, to be carved
out of stone and your
tears and the wars
(and the maps of the wars
that are the lines in them)
and the women who
have birthed you and
wed you and left you
and kindled your heart
to this burning red stone,

centuries have past...

> *the black jaguar*
> *sniffs the cage, pacing*

and I sit on the bed
in a small pink skirt
tornadoeing the white
sheets as I simmer and fret,

your voice, your far voice
intoxicating my cheeks, my
eyes with this immemorial
longing.

Come to me now,
my Beloved, and bring me
from the far world, from
the *quattro cento* detour
through cathedrals and
lapis, through mists
and blood,

your hands—
which I adore.

6

Epiphany

Just before dying we
will see it all, the weave
of the cloth, the pattern
of the whole tableau
obscured by life as we knew
it, "getting and spending," as
Amy said, war and work, gains
and losses, "relationships," as
we have known them: habits
of the human condition.

Just before dying, it
will all come clear, like
a digital photo, ripened
for two seconds, reveals the
moment that is already
gone forever.

Then, it will all make sense.
We will gasp at the stunning
astonishing grandeur of it all

and what we missed along
the way, clutching at moments
that seemed important—and were
important—at the time,

as this afternoon, suddenly
the grey clouds parted and a
mother and father bird, followed
by three speckled chicks, their
legs as thin as a hair,

walked across the spring
green lawn, and the phone
rang and your voice spoke
what we have come to call

"the true and beautiful things:"

> "I love you, and I've just
> made love to you in a dream.
> You're beautiful and
> strong, and you jump
> through space and time."

I too am alone here and far,
lost on this island of distant
blue waters, green turtles, beige
polyester golf hats and Bermuda
shorts, red Nike running shoes,
white crumbled plastic
boogie boards.

All our pasts have gathered
in this single life of beauty
and disaster, sorrow and
magnificence, where nothing
in the way the world works
works for us, and nevertheless
the gold light nets us
with its fire.

We've been at this a long
time now: Warrior/Queen
soldier/soldier, Joan of Arc and
the legions riding out from Blois.
I have married you and lost you
a thousand times already

> *strength and beauty*
> *power and magnificence*
> *strange love, wild fire*

And once again
we won't go on together—
not as the world sees going on,
under a single roof with walls and
television sets and garbage pails, the
days of our lives counted down
like the numbers of a rocket
launching at Cape Kennedy.

All these days of wondering
about you, thinking as the world
thinks, "Does he love me?" "Will he
call?" "What are we doing in this dance of
whiteness and insanity?" "How many times
will we deeply gorgeously fall and almost
touch, only to be sent back to
the void again?"

Lives like an afternoon thunder
shower: here, then gone; our love
immense and terrible, woven
through all our lovers and
strangers: this single vast
heart bleeding endlessly
open—

petals of roses
smeared on a sidewalk,
drowning in a summer rain.

7

When I Hold You

When I hold you I see
the thousands of beatings
crouched like whipped dogs
in your eyes. I see you

fall from the highchair and
the stairs and the tree, feel the
palms and knuckles across your
cheeks, the hands like a noose
around your neck,

the sorrow endless sorrow
rage endless rage, and
how none of them ever
could you trust.

When I hold you I feel
the sorrow I can't touch,
worlds of sorrow, lifetimes
of losses, hundreds of
deaths and severings:
blood and dust and the
pounding of hoofs on the
black earth beneath your
feet, the white bones
beneath your face.

When I hold you I feel war
and the sounds of war and
the thickness of death, grey felt
blankets stanched with blood,
ribbons of flesh hanging down
loose like fringes on a tablecloth.

When I hold you I see a
small boy walking beside a
running creek, dragonflies
and locusts, the sweet green
of crushed weeds under
your feet, the light in your
eyes already gone out,
your cry scorched, and
the words burned down
to cinders in your throat.

When I hold you I can feel
the gash, the oozing red
ravine in your heart for
which there are in all the
world not tourniquets
enough: stale blood
and crumbled tears:
ashes on a windowsill.

When I hold you I feel the
astonishing smoothness of your
skin, silk of your hair, strength
of your muscles and bones,
faint light brimming the blacks of
your eyes and in the prison of your ribs
your heart a dark vast weeping
cathedral beating with prayers.

When I hold you my body opens,
becomes a river for you, a clear
quarry pool for you to dive
into; my eyes become an
ocean for you, my arms
a boat to carry you home.
My breasts rise to offer these
two white hills for you to rest
in, the plain of my belly a
a place to come to.

When I hold you, your
tears fall out of my eyes.
I cry the ancient whimper in you.
My heart stumbles, and oh, with
this small voice and these little
hands I hold you, Beloved,
as well as I can.

When I hold you, I hold you
like a woman holds a man.

8

When You Hold Me

When you hold me I feel
the strength of a thousand
armies gathered around me,
taste the scent of protection
the whip and furl of hundreds
of colored banners being
carried across the field.

When you hold me I feel
exquisite, beautiful, a silver
chalice, a crystal vase, an alabaster
box intaglioed with crosses, and
inlaid with precious stones.

When you hold me, I feel
gathered and precious
and safe and small.
You loosen the tears
from my eyes like God
loosens the rain from the clouds,
and I shall rejoice when my tears
fall into the bowl of your hands.

When you hold me
I fall backward in time
to the balcony and the carriage:
hoofs chopping on cobbles
and the lanterns shifting in the dark:

> *ermine and taffeta and silk, vervaine*
> *and bergamot and chevrefeuille*
>
> *while in the half-light*
> *black-gloved and shivering*
> *the hand traces across the page.*

I have written you so many
letters, Beloved—

all those ancient burning
autumns and silent fires, and
the wind passing over the fields...

When you hold me
I lie in the bed in the castle,
drawing back the red heavy
curtains: scrape of twisted iron rings
against an iron rod: passion and death
and milk and blood. I smell the
sweat in your armor, taste the
dust in your hair, read the dark
remembrance of battle
in your eyes.

I have been waiting so long for
you...

Losing you, always losing
you, always going away
from you, missing you always:
tall ships with high masts, horses
carriages and battlefields...

Life after life the mists
rose, the boat sailed
the louvers closed
and your horse rose up
on its hind legs and turned
away in the early evening...

When you hold me,
clouds gather, tears fall
and you kiss them away, each
little one of them like the whole
lifetime of sorrow it is, blessing
me, caressing me, erasing all
the nameless years and
the way it has not been.

> *In the distance the castle rises.*
> *I sit again at the head of the table,*
> *wearing the long blue dress, looking down*
> *through the long double row of silver goblets*
> *to see you kneeling there with your sword…*

When you hold me I feel
sheltered and gathered and
treasured and claimed.
When you hold me you
hold me fiercely,

like a Warrior
holds a Queen.

9

Away From You

Three days of silence; the world
has fallen off its edge. I've eaten
too many carbohydrates, drunk
too much coffee and wine, watched
too many scudding clouds, the Detroit
River restlessly pawing its banks.

Too many centuries of this: the
heart, like the jawbone in the
dentist's office, wearies of being
held open without being fed, and yet
remains open, titillated with expectation
of what might follow—peace, well-being

or a kiss. Still, through these long hard
days—why did I come here anyway?
call it a business trip—you have
crowded my eyes with the onslaught
of yourself: that sword standing
ready in the corner of that woman's

house—roses falling apart
on the black glass surface of her
table as we talked. I longed for
you, feeling the narrow desperate
spindles of your breath in the spring
green leaves of the elms outside her
kitchen window, the memory of your
touch ascending the white thin
ladder of my spine

as it arranged itself in her
chair. How can I lose you again
so easily, after all these centuries,
of recording the polonaise of your
heartbeat in the spiraling luminous
strands of my DNA? The soul plays

tricks: hide and seek, here a life, there
a life, different costumes, suitors and
contenders for the throne. Down at
the bones of the soul we remember
it all, but it's such an excavation
always, sending the yellow canary

down the mine shaft to see if
it lives or dies of the fumes of
this particular life. I have waited
forever for you and I will wait
forever for you
again,

until we shudder together
in the landscape where no bird
flies, no song is necessary, the
wind neither rises nor falls,
kisses become us, the faint
intoxicating shadow of our
humanity haunts us like
a distant dream

and we live, in a spiral of
endless startling beauty,
the soul's white dance.

10

Time and Distance

Is love still love without
voices and hands, when the
time is not the same and the
geography has changed?

I called to whisper good-night
to you, this late night while the
footfalls of angels slippered
the sky and my heart, this
open abyss of embarrassment
and longing, this chalice of
endless breathless openness
awaits your everything.

Today the sun rose and fell
in midflight, besieged by
clouds, heavy rain. In hours
four seasons passed, moving
me from golden to a black
hole I know well, with just
the scrape of a thrush's

wing against the transparent
pane of this seamless window
called *Us*. Love once was having
and wanting, but now your
black shoes tread the earth
of my soul imprinting me
with the shape of your
soul's footfalls, with the
sound of them and even with
the memory of the sound
of them. Shoes and boots

and swords and reins, tools
of the millenniums, piercing
through whiteness and
sorrow—the lives in which we lost
everything, our houses
and children, the fields to
the fire and the beautiful
dances of coming into each
others' arms. It was all torn
down, melted and burned
and we rose, like a rose
from it time and again.

I write in my book as
the incense burns, the
violet flowers drop their
petals, the clock ticks
and the water shudders
in the glass. Give me your

skin, the wet depth of your
eyes and the horrors that
have laid you waste. I
crave you, crave all the
deaths that will bring you
back to me again, and the
liquid white infinite blossoms
that are aroused by your
kiss…

11

Letting Go

I, too, am letting go of things,
towels, old lovers, torn underwear,
my youth, my footing, that one
rust-colored tube of lipstick
I bought in Paris two years ago.

It's late, or should I say
too early in the game to know
just what we're doing here.

Tonight I've been carved
from my sleep by the sharp
white sword of the moon, and
I've come to the red room to write.

The candles are lit; in the distance
the train weaves its way down
the tracks to the grating of
trucks on the freeway.

Somewhere out there in
the dark, I can still feel you
letting go of old gym
bags, self-loathing
and the ordeal:

another wife, that house with
too many ruffles, six figure
pieces of furniture, the
wrong kind of
music.

I don't know where
I'm going, don't know
who I'm going with.

Is it you I wonder,
you of the thousand
lives and the endless wars
and the million farewells, you
with the soul-print of my soul
the way the hoof-print of the first
cloned lamb can double for its double,
you who with hands and words and
no words say everything?

Here we both are again,
back in in a life: blossoms
and anguish, and a
remembrance that sears.

And this is what love is—
a mirror that pierces through
to the core with its pure white
seeing, and memory just
a pattern on the tablecloth?

> *Castles and haymows*
> *stretchers at the edges*
> *of the battlefields, and winter*
> *nights so black, so riddled with*
> *stars and candlelight, making it*
> *clear as I looked down the table*
> *and saw you there kneeling*
> *with your sword, the terrible*
> *distance between us…*

I have lived and you
have died for me before…

Now, here, waiting again,
my heart carved open
with all this beauty, all
this sorrow, I am the
chalice, the wings and the womb,
and I am waiting again for you
as I have waited forever before:
at twilight, on the balcony, in the castle
at the head of the table, in the tents
at the edges of the battlefield...

The light fades; the thread grows thin
so that tracing the shadows of the shadows
at times becomes quite difficult...

> *the tree and the forest*
> *where once long ago*
> *you came riding. I was*
> *gathering mushrooms;*
> *you came to my basket;*
> *and we lay down together*
> *in the moss...*

Ah, yes, and there's
another one...

I suppose that
when we get down to the
bones we will know all our lives.
We will see that they were all made of
light, and that we were all made of light,

and that all the rest was just
a slowly revolving tableau.

But I have not yet been given
to see this, and so just for now
for just the time being, for just
this littlest moment called life

I am letting go of letting you go.
I am falling into the falling in.
I am waiting for you in the twilight
again and climbing in

to the living dream.

12

High Mirror

When I see how your fingers
fold and trace, soothe
and caress,

I see the white tips of my
fingers beating like two white
wings, palming your forehead
and eyes.

When I see the beauty of
your hands, the way they turn
and move and hold, gather my
neck like the green long stem of
a rose, tracing that ancient scream
in my throat, unleashing tears, I
think of my own hands, ruffling
hair, soothing losses,
unravelling pain.

When you say, "Thank you,"
and "Please" and "You're welcome,"
pausing, allowing these plain words
to fall like leaves in air, like
bandages on wounds,

I feel the simple sweetness
of my heart, my kindred kindness
and the true dimension
of my graciousness.

When I see how you
move, lunging and curling,
assaulting the earth with your
feet, slashing the air with your
sword, with your hard turns and
crosses and spirals,

I see the long grace
of my body in motion, the
crossed legs and dropped toes,
the gradual steady floating
across the room.

When I see the white pale
moon of your soul, the lingering
catastrophes of aeons parked
like an Explorer rocket on
its grey pock-marked
geography

and the sun of your heart, insanely
golden with joy, alive with the pure
aghast amazed receiving of every
small and beautiful thing,

I see the faint bright
glare of my own pretty soul
fluttering in the distance like
an invitation to the dance.

When I see your lips
how they gather to kiss
and open to reveal that
one small space between
your teeth that opens the door
through which your laughter
walks in,

I see the striped umbrella
of my smile, how many have
been sheltered beneath it,
how it has turned away
rain and scattered arguments.

I have waited, I say,
in the black ditch of not
knowing, through bad sentences,
stupid decisions, the long uninteresting
passage of time, ravaged by longing,
despairing, blind to the magnitude which
claimed becomes freedom and denied
is death, (like the chicken bone in
the throat that can kill you in a
minute in a restaurant),

wondering about
my own soul, it's exact and
singular dimensions, and whether
or not it would one day bloom in the
world—this world or any other—

> it's so easy to lose track of
> your soul, leave it off like a
> skin at the moment of birth,
> then try all your life to wiggle
> your way back into it again—

but you have shown me its exquisiteness.

And so, my Beloved, tenderly,
still with inveterate shyness—the lips
quiver and the heart can almost not
contain—I open to this summer, this
seeing, this single high mirror, this
single white blossom that has
created itself from all the water
in this oasis,

this *Us*.

13

This Photograph

I want to give you this
photograph of me at the
lake, taken the year before
you were born. See me in
my black watch plaid
bathing suit, holding little
Mike in one arm and with
the other reaching down and
holding Scotty by the hand.

Those beautiful boys!
Holding them, I was already
learning to hold you, the sand hot,
my arms golden with sunlight, and
the blue lake behind us, a vast
dream of the deep and
unseeable future.

I held Mikie right up
next to my new breasts,
gathering his small life close
to my heart, without thinking
"heart" or "life." It's just that
for them, then, I was there to

carry and hold, to know
them by hand. In the blue
nights I swam naked in the
dark moon-silvered lake
discovering skin, limbs
and wetness. That was

the summer I learned to dance,
learned to kiss under the moon,
in a row boat, tied on the long
wooden dock we rowed out from
at midnight, with Howie, who's
dead now, but then, patiently in

the living room taught me:
"Step, right, together, step.
It's the box step," he said,
Howie, who after dancing
died in some war, but only

after first asking me to a dance
at his college, to which because
I was only fourteen, it was two cities
away and other unmentionables
of course I couldn't go.

Snake grass and how cool
the sand was in the dark,
candlelight and checked
red tablecloths at the old hotel
on Black Lake, wooden rafters
smelling of wetness and
spilled beer and a waiter that
one night, deadly handsome and
wearing a white dish towel
wrapped tight around his waist—

he, too, must have been Italian,
given those eyes—and the way the
music that night tore into something
deep and unbloomed in me, the way
longing etched the seams of my pillows
and sheets, and the lake night air came

in through the screen door, while
pristine and sorrowful, propped
up on four white pillows, I read
Thomas Wolfe every night in
the thin mosquito-honed air.

I wish you had been there
then, instead of unborn, and
I wish I had been in Philadelphia
ten minutes later when you did
get born. I would have taken
you, and held you like I held
Mikie and Scotty that
summer, in my happy
golden arms.

14

Double Take

Thinking tonight of the
two of us at six, writing
our poems down in those
black and white speckled
notebooks, already speechless
dumb with the pain,
splattering out the truth

on the page in a world that
kept falling in on itself, leaving
us both with the broken
song that could only be

written down—for you
between beatings or the
memory of beatings: your
pristine malleable skull
formed blow by blow like
a sculpture with each little
indiscretion of childhood: not
washing your hands, forgetting
to say "Pardon me," I suppose,
and God only knows what else.

We were beaten together,
though you were beaten more
and in fact. For me it was the slow
kill, the gradual demolition of
the spirit with the wrecking ball
of his intractable depression,
and her aching bones.
I could always feel her
needing so much. And
the hopelessness of it all.

Pain is the middle name
of childhood. We swam
in that river, grasping
at straws, reaching for
sunlight with pencils
and pens and black and
white speckled notebooks
that could almost hold
the world steady with
their faint blue lines.

I still think of Valley Green
and the horses there near
the pond in spring, and a
gaggle of dragonflies flirting
with God, skimming over its
surface, and how that water,
still as a stone, could hold
the whole sky in its lens,

and how, even standing inside
all that beauty, there was still
so much to reclaim: for me
a trickle of blood once, sluicing
backwards out of the vein, into
the hand and onto the page,

and for you, whatever was still
left to feel after he yet again
cracked your skull and you once
again saw stars: real stars, I suppose,
and shapes of green, and kinds of leaves,
and the hilarious unpremeditated

witness of the sun still coming up
every morning. There are no drugs
to kill that pain. Only life and the
thousands of words we laid
down in our black and white
speckled notebooks.

Page after page we have grown
toward some gradual Yes.

Words were the angels around us.

15

Your Body is the Grave

Your body is the grave
of all your lives, each wound
a death from a life that cuts
to the quick of this one—battle
fields and enemies already turned
to dust, mists of sorrow rising
from miles of trampled earth
engraved across its surfaces.

Here in this white room—
and I must remark once again how
in this life all the rooms you have
come to are white—all the
bedclothes and blankets
and sheets, all the walls and
the buildings outside the
walls, seen raggedly at night
through the windows like
ghosts of dead civilizations,
and even your own spent
ancient bodies—are white.

Here, now, to this white room—
scent of incense and candles,
and in your armpits the fragrance
of all your old deaths, you
endlessly kissing, caressing
undressing me…

Here, to this room, I have brought all my
whiteness: white of white lotuses and
clematis, feathers of doves and alabaster
boxes, white onyx and opals and pearls
clouds and eggs and white embroidered blouses,
laces and handkerchiefs, plasters and gauzes, zinc
oxide, the white walls of houses on Santorini
Belladonna flowers, white rag content paper
paperwhite narcissus, white linens and
silk, the whites of blue eyes framing their
blueness in moonlight, rice paper lampshades
white shutters in the tropics, white sand near
blue water, light and the whiteness
of God—

From all this whiteness
I have brought the white lily of my body
to lay it down like a shroud
on your grave.

Here, in your white room, lying
beside you, kissing, whispering,
the moon a white round scar in
the window, and each of these wounds
an old death printed out on the
palimpsest of your body like a
telegram from the war department—

The moon swims, the birds
clatter outside in the palm fronds
and I rise on my elbow to kiss all your wounds,
all these wounds on your shoulders and arms, on
your back and the vast black and blue terrain of your
thighs, and finally this one great wound so close to your
heart, this wound which to you is only another postcard
from death to your flesh but to me is the lodestar
of all your sorrows. (I know it was only
a fencing match, an afternoon's duel
on a lawn in a park in Santa Fe, but
this wound is so wide and so red
and has bled so hard all afternoon
and is as ancient as your soul…)

There is so much
silence around you, so much
unspoken pain in all these wounds
gathered like bodies, dead from the field,
like fruit, heavy, ripe from the tree. You have
hid everything in these wounds. In this dried
blood and these ragged scars are all the words,
tears, paragraphs and syllables, ancient immemorial
howlings, tender adoring sentences of all your
livings and dyings: Warrior, Lover, Hero, Witness,
you with the body exemplar, the hands
that open and touch and heal
and caress, that kill
and lay waste.

I have come here tonight
simply to touch you, to brush
my lips across all your wounds
and to tell you that we have come
here again, to life, and to all this whiteness—
white of three hundred and twenty thread
count white sheets, white of my skirts, of my few
silver hairs, of the rims of my nails, of the lace on the
hems of my nightgowns, the square white tiles in
your kitchen, the high white shutters
here in your room—

We have come here, I say, to all this
whiteness, to let the words spill, and the
blood be spoken, the deaths be buried
and the everlasting life begin.

So come to me now, my Beloved,
Let me kiss all your wounds and bury all your
old deaths in the sweet curved casket of my neck.
Let your howl rise up through the white ravine
between my breasts, your tears run
down like a river though it.

When love kisses death
all heaven breaks open.

Surrender. Fall Forward. Begin!

16

The Italian Fountain Pen

This morning in the scraped grey
dawn, after the candles and your
thighs, you gave me the pen:
onyx, with the golden nib
numbered on the lid of
the box with the numbers
of our two souls.

I have written you down
the centuries, your dark
eyes piercing the sullen
black nights:

> *Oh, God, it's the*
> *balcony again, and*
> *your horse, scent of*
> *pomander and jasmine*
> *and the thousand dried*
> *tears: frozen crystals paving*
> *the hem of my dress…*

And then last night
I came into your rooms,
especially that one white
room we walked so easily into,
up the stairs, against an explosion
of palm trees and fiberglass awnings
the night cry of television
screams, piercing the
yellow-black horizon.

Here is the water
in a ringed glass.
Here is the photograph
of the martial artist. Here
are the pewter candlesticks
on the dining room table, the bad
art on the north wall and the
substance of your body,
shimmering, alive with
wounds, and glistening
with pain.

"We've had minutes,
only, always." You said
that as no clock ticked, but
centuries unraveled between
our lips and thighs:

> *guns and smoke in the*
> *distance, dead horses*
> *splayed out on the field,*
> *and cities driven*
> *into the ground,*
> *as garment by*
> *garment we tore*
> *back time*
>
> *Ah, yes…*
> *Ah, this…*

and how the leg remembers
your calves and my head
finds once again its cradle
in your shoulder bones

scent of musk and
juniper, wet velvet and blue
stones, white steel and chrysophase
mercury and jute and amber

and how, always, kiss by kiss, I have held
all these words for you, this vast encyclopedia
of sorrow and of memory: passion and loss,
loss and passion:

how we were and
where we were and
what, each time, before the war
we said to one another.

Oh, my Warrior!

Memory, that catastrophe
in my heart, dismantled through
the thousand black nights of all our snapped
lives, rises again with the moon, as once
again, we meet and touch.

And so the night passed.

the mystery crawls
across the centuries,
an old wild-eyed dog
dragging toward home

The moon falls, the sun comes,
and as we sit on the couch in the blue
brittle morning, you hand me the box,
which, without the genius of
your hands, I cannot open.

Finally, the lid springs loose
and there, in the sarcophagus
of all our hopes and passion
lies the Italian fountain pen
made of white onyx and
obsidian and gold.

I lift it, turning the wide stone
barrel slowly in my hand:

You have given me the
instrument that holds
the words for all our lives

and I will write them down.

17

What She Wrote

With the Italian pen,
given to her by the Italian,
she has written in the
Italian notebook:

"I am so sad that
once again, I have only
these flickering moments
with you,

sad that I come
to and run from
your beauty, sad

I can't move
into the river of
feelings with you,

that my mouth seems
always to be full of
stones, my throat
with cotton wool, old
gauzes full of blood,

sad that the way,
whatever the hell it
might be, isn't open,

sad that I lie in your
bed, in your immense
and gathering arms, your
wounded, war-making
arms, and feel like a

visitor, an impostrice,
one whose soul has
been here for all
eternity, but whose
body endlessly comes
and goes: white,
hungry, wanting.

I'm sad I can't
talk to you with
real words, with the
beautiful wisdom I
give from the chair,
with the whispered
delicious encouraging
words I can give when
my body has been
ravished, my soul
has come to the
place it can
come to.

> *I'm lost.*
> *Hold me.*

I'm sad, again, for all
the years. I want to
scream about the endless
horrible weirdness, out-
of-syncness, mysterious
duplicitous and hence
lying miraculous con-
vergence of our selves.

I don't trust—any
thing or anyone.

Hold me.

Let your arms
which have lived
and died a thousand times
and are stronger than God
prove something.

I don't want to go
anywhere new, any
where else. It all, always
ends in pain. Another
good-bye, the hell
of withdrawal and lament
and starting over, broken
a little bit more, some
where else. With
someone else.

I don't care about
the broken—that's probably
a lie. I care about the
someone else, the some
where else, the hell of
not trusting and not,
yet again, being able to
come home.

Home… is
a phantom.

Perfection is something
that must not be sought.
Peace, I suppose, is living
in the anguished—no, the
anguishing—ambivalence
of the anguishing ambi-
valence. Surrendering
to the fucking ambi-
valence. The endless
fucking ambivalence.

Maybe I don't take a
stand because there's
no fucking stand to take.

> *If there is a stand*
> *where the hell is it?*

I've got to get off
this goddamn endless
emotional monologue,

Some steadiness
somewhere,

"Please, God."

18

Dinner with Will

Sitting in the Star Anise with
Will, looking out from the
back wall—like Ingrid Bergman
I always like to sit near the
wall (Anderson said
that)—and looking
out at the ochre and
violet and emerald green
planes of the walls that they
had arranged in triangles, the
gold-leaf framed niches,
the huge bouquets of
ginger flowers and orchids
(lacking only the geckos) and
those plates of green rice noodles
rising like miniature air-borne
intestines from white platters
on the high shelf behind
which the cooks were
searing the salmon—

Sitting with Will, wearing white
as I usually do, (but tonight
draped also with a red fringed
cashmere cape), watching him
lift his glass of red Zinfandel and
noticing how finally, at fifty-two,
age is starting to have her way
with him, especially around
the eyes; I listened while he
spoke of not loving enough
the girl he is fucking (as
he put it) and imagining
sometime a love that
would defy, erase
all that.

"It would be a soul love," he
said, twisting the stem of the
glass in his fingers—hands
I have watched grow lines,
drop wedding rings for more
than twenty years now, beautiful
they were when I first met
them, smooth, well-formed
and sensitive, the tips of their
fingers primed for touching—

"A soul connection," he reiterated,
"and all the categories you set—
whether she was tall or could
dance or had children or money
or dogs—would dissolve. The love
would just cut through you to the core,
and your whole life would be
rearranged in an instant."

"But what would you do,"
I asked him, "in real life, on
Tuesdays and Wednesdays
and Thursdays?" "I don't know,"
he said. He set his glass back down
on the table as if setting a ballerina
very carefully back down on
the stage. "Maybe we would
go fishing. Or I would go
fishing. And she would
stay home and write.

"It wouldn't matter.
It wouldn't be about Wednesdays
and Thursdays. It would be about love.
It would be a true and beautiful thing,
and I've been waiting for it my whole
life. I don't understand you," he said,
finally, looking at me, irritated. "I
think you know what I mean."
Then he waved at the waitress
for another glass of wine.

On the polished cement floor
the sound of her footsteps
like hoofbeats approaching…

I thought of you then.

19

How You Came In

Through the wrong door.
Inconveniently. It was spring.
Those yellow flowers were already
blooming in the yard. I had been waiting,
dressing, though not in white, for the occasion.
Walked out to meet you on the porch.
Shook, as I recall, your hand.
Sat with you. Listened.
All that.

> *"It's hard for spirits, too," Michael,*
> *the seer, said that, after the first little*
> *stroke, lying curled up on the floor, dying*
> *of AIDS, his psychic vision clearer than*
> *ever, meaning, I think, that spirits, too,*
> *have trouble, in the material world,*
> *trying to get their message across.*

I regretted—and not—the wrong
door, my green dress. And how again,
already, we were doomed, consigned to
another fucking hopeless configuration.
The balcony. And the carriage.
And the castle. It just goes on
and on, doesn't it?
And now the chair:

"Where were you born?"
"Philadelphia. And you?"
"Philadelphia. What did
they do to you?"

"The same."

Then, of course, there were
your hands and the shirt
(*sans* sleeves) and your body
stilettoed with rage from all
those wars, and that tattoo of a
fish on your shoulder. Fishing
on Tuesdays. Of course.

How many times have
we lain in the spent dawn
knowing it was the last hour
or the only hour, feeling the war
that still isn't over or is
just about to begin?

Shrapnel and fireflies and
doubt, and the thousands of
reasons why not. Lotuses, wisteria
and salt, and the movement of your hands
through the quarries of time—
and in the back room miles
of white dresses folded
and waiting.

> *There is no one left here
> to talk to. The lights have all gone
> out in the city. Carrier pigeon, Morse code,
> computer print-out and screen, and a
> computer-illiterate angel trying to
> get his message across…*

(Always the backward
step to go forward: the pit
reaches up with its arms
to embrace.)

Then the light pierces, a crocus through snow:
you didn't come here so I could heal you,
you came so you could find me again.
The wrong door, in this life, was the only
way in. There was no balcony this time.
And the forests have all been
excised from the map.

>*"It's hard, too, for spirits,"*
>*Michael said that, lying folded*
>*origami-like on his black and white*
>*kitchen linoleum floor, a final*
>*pronouncement before*
>*becoming a spirit*
>*himself...*

And so you came in, as I said,
through the wrong door. Because
this is the end. It's the last call, the
eleventh hour. The war is over.
The boats have already sailed.
Exhume the sarcophagus,
kill off the funeral pyre.

Backward, forward and sideways,
this time we are rowing toward Love.

20

The Wife You Are Leaving

I just passed the beach where you first met
her. Under black sky I sat on grey sand.
The water roiled and collided around
me, roaring me backward and
sideways through time.

Clouds parted, mists
rose, and I saw her then
after I left you, when I
was laid out in that gilded
casket, holding two white lilies
in my hands: all memory of The
Table gone, and the chattering lapis
taffeta dress, and my eyes looking
down through the long double row
of silver goblets, to see you kneeling
there in the dark, your armor a shadow
of sorrow around you, your sword
awash in the candlelight.

Gone, gone, the chiarascuro of
your face, and how you kneeled
and your black eyes gleamed. Gone,
too, the memory of your breath,
that hovered like a spring wind
always, arising the hairs on
the nape of my neck.

Suddenly, I could see it all,
how after I died you rode in on your
horse, roared into the cathedral reeling,
your howl rising up to the clerestory
windows. "How could she die while I
was out dying for her?!" you screamed
tearing your sword from its scabbard
swearing that you would fall on it,

while the censors shuddered
with oil and ash, fire and light,
my profile frozen under glass,
tips of these fingers never again
to touch your face, your risen
scepter ever again.

How she, my competitor,
peeled you back from the brink of death,
dragged you away in her long strong arms
black-sheathed with envy and mourning.
How she formed you, set you
back into life again,

How she inherited you from a queen—

raging, angry, that her hard strength
could never make her queenly.

And yet I know that she loved you strong—
not with tears, yours or hers—but with
steadfastness, and a will to win.

We have been dancing down these
stones for aeons, dying old and
dying young, and every time
she has wormed her way in,

dragging you back to the sword
and the war, gluing you back
to life and herself, a single
battle at a time.

Of such was her love.

Tonight, in the sand where you
first met, I pause to salute her—
she who rode you back to the war
and held you to the grindstone of life,
when I was a lily snapped from its stem,
singed untimely brown from white.

We are all light in the end,
but here in the middle, I, the lily and she
the lion, the two of us have taken turns, holding
you and being held, lying with you in tangled
sheets perfumed with your sweat and blood
willing you off to war again, waiting,
aching for your return.

I have loved you with my royal heart
and this, I know, is my single strength.
Life after life, I have blossomed at your
touch and held your wounds as sacred,
precious, worthy beyond words.

I died then, young and a queen, but
in this life I rise for you from the casket,
bearing two white lilies in my hand.

21

Sometime Later

Sometime, later, we will
remember all this in silence.
It will be spelled out in the
strange lights in our eyes, read
unexpectedly in airports, in the
lobbies of foreign hotels.

The air will suddenly stand
still around us and they'll ask,
"What happened, Darling?"
"Sweetheart, are you alright?"

Through loudspeakers
announcing the last flights
to Paris, desk clerks assigning
the rooms in which, with someone
else we will each spend the
night, we will hear
something…

> *the sound of bare hoofs*
> *on cobbles, whitewashed in*
> *moonlight, the drawing back*
> *of red heavy curtains: twisted*
> *rings on iron rods, the passage*
> *of a satin hem across*
> *a marble floor.*

I don't know how
we'll get there from here,
through what blood or petal
strewn paths, how many phone
calls and credit card bills, black
nights at the edges of how
many oceans it will take
for us to lose and find
each other once again.

It's such a journey
of beauty and anguish
here, on the dance floor
of life. So open your arms,
my Beloved; let my hair fall
like white wings on your
shoulders and the
stunned moon

caress us awake asleep awake
again, until in some life
after this one

> *knives and faucets and*
> *spaceships, razor blades*
> *and maidenhair ferns*

we shall awake
to one another
once again.

22

Enfin

Where shall I begin?
In a new notebook
with the Italian pen?
In the garden of men
blooming in the pink
sunset, none of them
close enough to touch,
their minds like alligators
gnawing at swamp grass

teeth bared and intelligent
waiting to break through
to something? My life

is this endless meditation
on losses: a minute here,
a minute there, the promising
rose smashed by the railroad
train, petals flattened into
steel. No pain, only the
solemn illicit rosebreath

creaking its last while
the train pulls out of the
station. Going nowhere
in particular. To the next
thing, whatever the hell
it may be, next ecstatic
encounter on 320 thread
count white sheets, next
pipe full of hash, sky full
of fireworks, bucket of
blood in the morgue.

Love come and goes
like the sound of the
train just past midnight
the moth wing frozen to
fire on the side of the
lamp. We burn to be born,
break open to open, and
all these deaths accrue
like jewels in the heart.

Letting go of it all once again:
breath and dreams, and a certain
smell of eucalyptus, the sound
of the summer screen door
closing. Nothing continues
not even the river, and it is
this walking into the water
endlessly of loss that
blesses us back
to the light:

It is good to have lost
you again—and loved.

After

After

Seeing you now
years after, the
weight of it all
engraved in your face
and how your hands
also, have changed,
grown lines—

We walk the beach
silent, awkward, fallen
finally into the lives that
we have chosen for this
life. The waves roar up,
breaking their backs
in our faces,

my tears a string
of beads to pray on.
As you said that one
night in those tall white
rooms, "we've had
minutes only,
always."

"Yes. And once again."

I long for death
for the seamless
infinite always
in which at last
with your beautiful
handless hands

you will wipe
endlessly
my tears away.

Postscript

We will remember always

in silence or in
the looks of our eyes

the days that we passed here,

How we called to one another
through the veil,

And how we laughed and cried.

Acknowledgements

Love and gratitude to my mother (in heaven) for providing the black and white speckled notebook and to my father (in heaven) for teaching me words every night after dinner; to Newt Wayland (in heaven) for igniting my poetry writing, to Les Wolf (also in heaven) for confirming it, and to FX Feeney, (happily still on earth) for being my literary champion and companion.

Deep gratitude to Judy Varga for being the clear-minded, large-hearted early editor of this work, and to Rita Tanos for creating the Satsang Salon at which many of these poems were first read.

Love, gratitude and appreciation to my daughter Molly Stuart for encouraging me to read my poems at the Sacramento Poetry Center—and for all our everythings.

Immense and heartfelt thanks to Bo von Hohenlohe for being the mighty encourager, relentless stickler for detail, and five-star general of forward movement in the process of transforming this book from a languishing manuscript to a breathing reality, and to John Ridland for the ballast of encouragement along the way.

I am blessed. I am grateful.

About the Author

Daphne Rose Kingma has been writing poetry since she was seven. She has won numerous prizes for her poetry and fiction, and her poems have been published in *Spectrum, Loci, The Kansas Quarterly, The New York Quarterly, and Prairie Schooner*. Sidetracked (and elevated) by a more than thirty year career as a psychotherapist, she is also the author of a dozen books about love and relationships, including the best sellers *Coming Apart, The Men We Never Knew, The Book of Love, Heart and Soul, The Future of Love*, and the prize-winning *The Ten Things To Do When Your Life Falls Apart*. Her first book of fiction, *The Magical World of Madame Metier*, will be published Spring, 2017, by Skyhorse/Perseus, NY. She lives in Santa Barbara, California.

For further information please visit www.daphnekingma.com